KNOW YOUR SPORT

Fishing

Rita Storey

First published in 2009 by
Franklin Watts
338 Euston Road
London NW1 3BH

Franklin Watts Australia
Level 17/207 Kent Street
Sydney NSW 2000

© Franklin Watts 2009
Series editor: Jeremy Smith
Art director: Jonathan Hair

**Series designed and created for
Franklin Watts by Storeybooks.**
Designer: Rita Storey
Editor: Nicola Edwards
Photography: Tudor Photography,
    Banbury
Advisor: Brian Syde

A CIP catalogue record for this book
is availablefrom the British Library.

Dewey classification: 799.1
ISBN 978 0 7496 8861 5
Printed in China

Franklin Watts is a division of Hachette
Children's Books, an Hachette UK company.
www.hachette.co.uk

Note: At the time of going to press, the statistics in this book were up to date. However, it is possible because of the anglers' ongoing participation in the sport that some of these may now be out of date.

Picture credits
The Print Collector/Alamy p6, © Paul Broadbent/Alamy p22; i-stock pp6 (bottom), 7, 8 (top right), 11, 15 (top right), 16, 19 (top and bottom right), 21 (top right), 23, 25 (top right) and 27; Tudor Photography pp3, 8 (bottom), 9, 11 (bottom), 12, 13, 18, 19 (bottom left), 20, 21 (right), 24, 25 (left), 26.

Cover images: Tudor Photography, Banbury.

All photos posed by models. Thanks to George Oakey, Luke Stratford and Megan Whitehouse

Taking part in any
sport has an element of risk.
Fishing can be dangerous if you
do not take the correct
precautions. Read pages 8 and 9
on Fishing Safety before
you start. If you are spending
time on or near water it is vital
that you know how to swim.

Contents

What is Fishing?

Fishing, also called angling, is the action of catching fish. People catch fish for food as well as for pleasure. Fishing is also a competitive sport. Catching fish requires skill, judgement and also an element of luck. It takes a lot of patience too. For many people the enjoyment of spending time outdoors catching fish is its own reward. Others relish the thrill of finding and landing big fish and enjoy competing in fishing as a sport. Fishing is a popular sport all over the world.

Fishing often takes place in beautiful and tranquil surroundings.

Fishing for Food

Fishing as a means of hunting for food is a practice that goes back over 40,000 years. Humans in all parts of the world have a history of fishing. Ancient people used nets, spears and stone hooks to catch fish. Ancient Egyptian documents and tomb decorations show people fishing in the River Nile. Over a thousand years ago, the Vikings caught and traded cod, an ocean fish.

This gold statue of Tutankhamun from the 14th century BCE shows him spearing fish from a reed boat.

Fishing for Sport and Fun

Sport fishing as we know it now began in the late 1600s. Anglers, or people who fish for sport or for fun, use some form of rod, reel, line and hook to catch freshwater or saltwater fish.

Different Types of Fishing

There are the three main categories of sport and recreational fishing.

Sea fishing: catching saltwater fish from the shore or from a boat.

Game fishing: fishing for salmon or trout. There are two types of game fishing – fly fishing and bait fishing.

Coarse fishing: fishing for freshwater fish except salmon and trout. Coarse fishing is the most popular type of fishing and it is the type this book will focus on.

Relaxation or Competition?

People who fish for pleasure do so to relax and enjoy their surroundings and the challenge of catching a fish. Anglers may return a fish to the water after logging its weight and measurements (this is called catch and release). Alternatively, they may take it home and cook it for dinner. Anglers who take part in sport fishing enter competitions, called matches, to catch fish under strict rules. The winners are awarded cups and prizes.

Fishing Clubs

Joining a fishing club is a good way to learn more about fishing in your local area. Fishing clubs often run competitions that are open to all ages. They stock their lake or pond before the competition so that there are plenty of fish to catch. Fishing competitions are fun, and spending time with other anglers can help you learn from their experience.

Anglers record the weight and measurement of the fish they catch.

Fishing Safety

Fishing is a relaxing sport but it has elements of danger too. You need to think ahead and plan your fishing to make it safe as well as fun.

Protecting the Environment

People who fish spend a lot of time by the sides of lakes, on riverbanks or by the sea. They must make sure that their activities do not harm these environments which are important habitats for wildlife. Animals and birds can die if they become caught up in discarded fishing lines or be badly injured by hooks left lying around.

Dos and Don'ts

Do use barbless hooks (see page 11).
Do be aware of wildlife around you and act to protect it. For example, retrieve your line if there is a risk of birds swimming through it.
Do protect yourself. Most places where you will be fishing will be owned by an angling club or private landowner. There will be a list of rules for you to follow to keep you safe.

Don't leave rubbish lying around, either while you are fishing or when you leave. Use the bins provided at angling clubs. If there is no bin available take everything home.
Don't leave baited hooks on the bank.
Don't leave your fishing rod unattended.

▲ A bird that became tangled in this fishing line would almost certainly die.

Fishing Hint

Do not use floating baits if swans and ducks are on the water, as they will take the bait and become caught on the hook.

Keep your mobile phone on silent or vibrate mode. ▶

Things to Take

Fishing is an all-weather activity, but you still need to think about the weather conditions when you plan your fishing expedition.

In cold or wet weather you will need:
- Plenty of layers of clothing to keep you warm and dry.
- Sturdy shoes or wellington boots to keep your feet dry and stop you slipping.
- An umbrella to keep the rain off.

In hot weather you will need:
- Sunscreen
- An umbrella for shade
- Drinks
- Insect repellent
- Sunglasses.

In hot weather it may be best to fish early in the morning or late in the evening as fish can be harder to catch in the heat of the day.

In all weathers you will need:
- A first aid kit
- Medicated wet wipes
- Something you can use to cut your fishing line if it gets tangled with birds or weeds.

- A mobile phone to let people know where you are.
- A lifejacket if you are sea fishing from a boat.

Things to remember on every fishing trip:
- Look around before you cast to check that nobody is behind you.
- Avoid wet rocks and steep slopes.
- Never walk out onto frozen water.
- Let someone know where you are or, better still, fish with a friend or an adult.
- Don't fish during thunderstorms as your fishing rod could attract a lightning strike.
- Keep away from overhead power cables as carbon fibre rods and poles are good conductors of electricity. Keep 30 metres from overhead lines.
- Canal and lake water can contain harmful bacteria. So before you eat, wipe your hands with a medicated wet wipe and cover cuts and grazes with waterproof plasters. Don't put line that has been in the water in your mouth when you are tying knots.

Keep a first aid kit handy to deal with minor cuts and injuries.

Fishing Equipment

It may seem as if there is a daunting array of fishing equipment, or tackle, for sale. When you're starting out, just buy a few pieces of basic equipment. You can always add more later.

Offering Bait

To tempt a fish to take a hook you need to offer it food called bait (see page 16). You use a rod or pole to get the bait near to the fish. You will also need a variety of floats and weights to position the bait at the level in the water where the fish can find it.

Getting Bait to the Fish

▼ **Floats** There are many different types of float to choose from. The waggler float is the most commonly used as it is suitable for most types of fishing. It is attached to the line at the base. It has a brightly coloured tip so that you can see it at a distance.

Waggler float

Fishing rod There are many different rods available. Some are specially designed for catching certain types of fish. To start with you can buy a general-purpose float rod. These rods are about four metres long and are quite lightweight. An alternative to a fishing rod is a pole (see page 24).

Equipment for Coarse Fishing

There are two main types of coarse fishing:
Float Fishing This is the most common type of coarse fishing. Anglers use a float to hold the bait at different depths in the water. A float holds the hook and bait in the water and stops them from sinking. To balance the float and keep it upright, small metal weights called split shot are attached to the line. When a fish bites, the float bobs under the water. The float, hook and line are called the rig.
Ledgering Fish that feed on the bottom of a river or lake are difficult to catch with a normal float rig. To catch this type of fish you need to use a technique called ledgering. A ledger is a weight attached to the line to hold the bait on the bottom. Ledgering is used in deep water and for fishing at a distance.

▼ **Split shot** The correct size of split shot to use is printed on the side of the float.

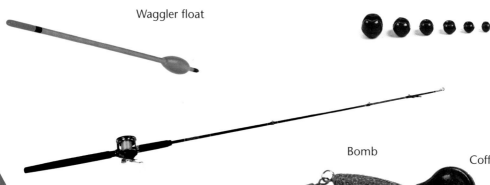

Bomb

Coffin

Bullet

Ledger weights Different types of ledger include bombs, bullets and coffins.

Hooking and Landing a Fish

Fishing line ▶

Hooks A barbless hook (left) and a barbed hook (right).

◀ **Reel** A fixed spool reel

Hooking and Landing a Fish

Hooks These come in two types, either 'eyed' or with a 'spade-end'. There are different sizes for different baits and for catching different fish. Some hooks have a backward facing 'barb' to stop the hook pulling out. Barbless hooks are recommended for catch and release fishing as they are easier to remove and cause less stress to the fish.

Line Fishing line is available in a variety of strengths, depending on whether you are float fishing or ledger fishing. You need to wind the line carefully onto the spool so that it will run freely.

Reel A fixed spool reel is the best type for beginners. It is easy to use and comes in different sizes. The spool has a 'drag' that you turn to allow you to let out the line when there is a fish on the hook. This stops the line breaking if the fish is pulling hard. Larger reels hold more line, which is useful if you are fishing for stronger fish such as barbel or carp.

Landing net A net for landing your fish onto the bank.

Disgorger A device for removing the hook from the mouth of a fish.

Keep net A net that stays in the water and is used for keeping the fish you have caught. You will need a keep net if you are fishing in a competition so that your day's catch can be weighed.

Get Organised

A baitbox will keep your bait in place and a well organised tackle box will ensure that everything you need is always to hand. As well as equipment for catching fish, you might like to take a tape measure, weighing scales and a camera with you so that you can record the details of the fish you catch.

▲ A well stocked tackle box.

Setting Up

Before you start fishing, you need to prepare the tackle and the bait you will need. Think about the weather conditions and have a good look around the area you will be fishing in (called the swim) to help you decide which bait and tackle to use.

Get Hooked!

In the UK, if you are over the age of 12 you will need to buy an Environment Agency rod licence before you fish. You will also need to get the permission of the owner of the water you want to fish.

Setting up a Float Rig: Stage 1

1. Fix the sections of your rod together.

2. Make sure that all the guide rings on the rod sections line up.

3. Attach the reel to the rod. Line up the spool with the first guide ring.

4. Open the bale-arm of the reel.

5. Thread the line through all the guide rings.

Setting up a Float Rig: Stage 2

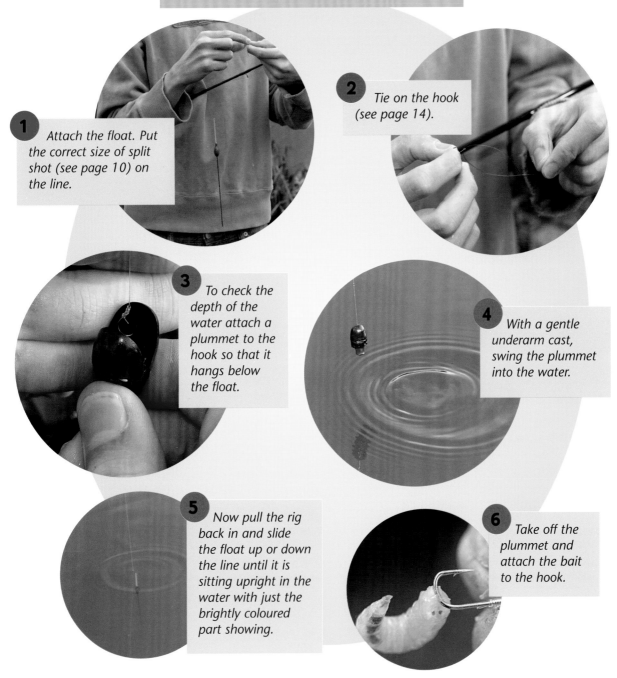

1 Attach the float. Put the correct size of split shot (see page 10) on the line.

2 Tie on the hook (see page 14).

3 To check the depth of the water attach a plummet to the hook so that it hangs below the float.

4 With a gentle underarm cast, swing the plummet into the water.

5 Now pull the rig back in and slide the float up or down the line until it is sitting upright in the water with just the brightly coloured part showing.

6 Take off the plummet and attach the bait to the hook.

Before You Start

Once you have set up your rig you are almost ready to fish. Make sure that you have all the things you are likely to need close by, such as your landing net and extra bait. Throw in some loose bait to attract the fish, stay still and quiet and be prepared for a fish to bite.

Knots

If you tie a knot incorrectly a struggling fish can escape. Practise some basic knots so that you can be sure of getting them right every time.

Figure of Eight Knot
This knot is used to attach a length of line with a hook on it, onto a fishing line.

Half Blood Knot
This is a very strong multi-purpose knot. Its main use is to attach hooks to the main line.

Figure of Eight Knot

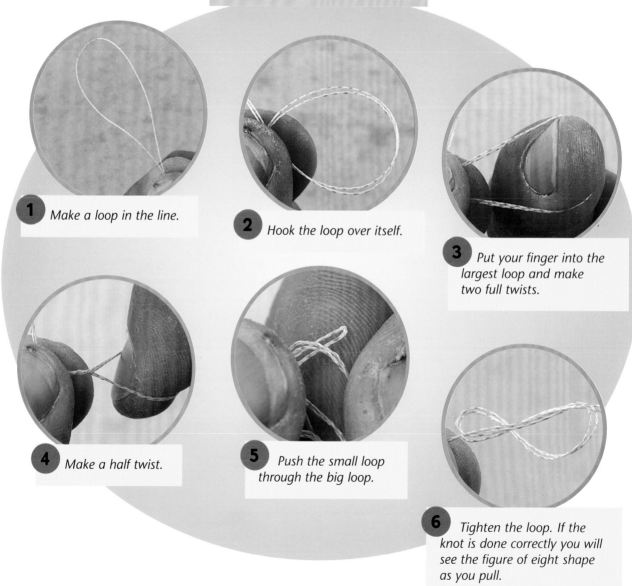

1 Make a loop in the line.

2 Hook the loop over itself.

3 Put your finger into the largest loop and make two full twists.

4 Make a half twist.

5 Push the small loop through the big loop.

6 Tighten the loop. If the knot is done correctly you will see the figure of eight shape as you pull.

Half Blood Knot

1 Thread the line through the eye. Double it over to make a loop.

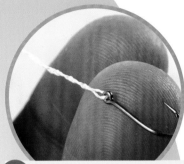

2 Hold it tight and make eight twists in the line.

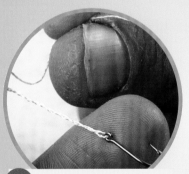

3 Take the loose end and thread it through the loop between the top of the hook and the first twist.

4 Thread the loose end back through the loop that is formed.

Roach

Appearance
Roach have a red iris, giving them the nickname 'redeye'.

Where to find roach
Roach can live in a wide range of conditions and are widespread in the UK and across the whole of Europe.

When to fish for roach
Roach are active throughout the year, even in cold weather. They are most active at dawn and dusk but they feed throughout the day.

How to fish for roach
The most popular methods are float fishing with a waggler float (see page 10) and ledgering using a swimfeeder (a tube filled with bait that is released gradually into the water).

Bait
Maggots, casters and bread.

5 Gradually pull the knot tight so that it is just above the eye of the hook. Trim off the extra line.

Bait

To catch a fish you need bait to tempt it on to your hook. There are many different types of bait to choose from.

Natural Bait

Worms

Redworms – good for catching perch, roach, and especially bream.

Lobworms – good bait for large fish.

Dendrobaena (also known as nightcrawlers) – a very wriggly worm on the hook which makes it a particularly effective bait.

Grubs

Grubs are the lava of flies. They are the most popular bait for coarse fishing. They stay on the hook well and most freshwater fish will take them.

Maggots – the grubs of bluebottle flies. They come in different colours and some species of fish may prefer one colour to another. After three or four days maggots turn into chrysalises. Called casters by anglers, these chrysalises are used to catch roach, dace, tench and bream.

Pinkies – the grubs of greenbottle flies. About half the size of a maggot, these are used to catch smaller fish.

Squatts – the grubs of houseflies. Useful for catching fairly small fish.

Natural Bait

Worms

Lobworms

Redworms

Dendrobaena

Grubs

Maggots

Squatts

Pinkies

Cupboard Bait

Bread

Dog biscuits

Sweetcorn

Cheese

Luncheon meat

Cupboard Bait

These are foods that you can buy from supermarkets and may already have in your kitchen cupboard:

Bread – useful for catching a variety of species but particularly for carp and tench.

Cheese – this can be moulded onto the hook and it stays on longer than some other baits. Cheese is particularly useful for catching chub – some say the smellier the better!

Luncheon meat/chopped ham or pork – used to catch coarse fish, particularly barbel.

Sweetcorn – a good all-purpose bait.

Dog biscuits – seriously! Some fishermen use them for catching carp in the summer.

Tackleshop Bait

Groundbait – this is a breadcrumb-like mixture which you scatter over the water to tempt fish into the area you are fishing. You can add some of the bait that you are putting on the hook into the groundbait as well.

Boilies – a powdered bait that is rolled into balls and boiled. You can buy these ready-made in a variety of flavours or make your own using a powder mix. Good for big fish.

Deadbait – dead minnows and young roach can be used as bait to catch large predatory fish, such as pike, catfish, zander or eels.

Tackleshop Bait

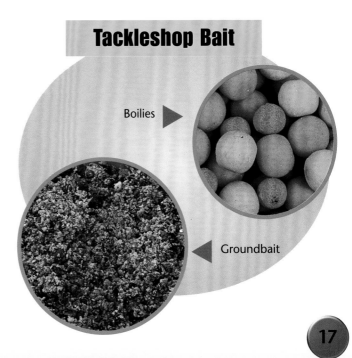

Boilies

Groundbait

Finding the Fish

To be a successful angler you need to find out where different species of fish live and know their habits and how they behave. You are like a detective looking for clues to help you find the fish and work out ways of catching them.

Ask Around

Joining a fishing club is a good way to meet other anglers in your area. Experienced anglers are usually happy to talk to younger members of the sport and pass on their knowledge. Tackle shops are also good sources of information. Ask what types of fish are stocked in which locations. Get some tips on how to find fish and the best bait and rig to use.

Look Around

Before you decide where to fish, look at the water and the surrounding banks. Look for signs, such as bubbles or ripples on the water, to help you work out where the fish are. Watch what other anglers are doing and see how successful they are. Learning to read a river takes time and patience but it is a skill that can help you to catch more fish.

Think Like a Fish

Fish do not want to be caught, they want to feed safely away from predators, such as bigger fish – and you! Fish can often be found in inaccessible places such as under tree roots or low overhanging branches, in weeds and around rocks. Predatory fish hide in slow flowing water waiting for small fish to swim past so that they can dart out and catch them.

The time of day and the temperature of the water in the swim will affect where the fish will be feeding. These factors will determine the rig and bait that you use.

This fishing lake is stocked with carp, tench, roach, bream, chubb, rudd, pike and perch. Carp are found close to the island and the nearside bank. Pike and perch are in the reeds and under tree roots. Tench are found deep down in the water. All the other fish are in the open water.

◀ Passing boats can make canal fishing difficult.

◀ Feeding fish are often found where side streams join main rivers and under bridges where it is dark.

Perch

Appearance
Young perch are easily identified by their dark stripes. The dorsal fin is spiny and its other fins are a bright orangey-red. Older fish are less brightly coloured.

Where to find perch
Perch are found in most parts of Europe in rivers, ponds, lakes, lochs and canals.

When to fish for perch
All year round, but in deeper water in the winter.

How to fish for perch
Float fishing and ledgering are both effective. Perch like to hide in weed beds, under tree roots and beneath overhanging trees.

Bait
Lobworms, maggots, casters, cheese, luncheon meat, bread, sweetcorn. Deadbait such as minnows can also be used as perch are carnivores.

Hook
6–14 depending on the bait you choose.

Line
4lb

Still Water

Perhaps the easiest type of fishing is in a lake or pond. This water is still and there is no current. Angling clubs and private landowners often stock fishing ponds and lakes with a range of fish such as perch, roach, bream, pike and carp.

Flowing Water

Rivers and canals are good places to fish. Rivers are usually deeper than canals and faster flowing. In moving water the fish may be nearer the bank or deep down in the water. Water in a canal usually moves more slowly, which some species of fish prefer. However, in the summer the number of boats on a canal may make fishing conditions difficult.

Casting

The aim of casting is to get the hook into the water as close as possible to where you think the fish might be. Casting is all about timing the release of the line at exactly the right moment. Learning to cast accurately takes a lot of practice.

There are many different ways of casting. The instructions given here are for a basic overhead cast with a fixed spool reel. This type of cast is suitable for both float and ledger tackle.

Anglers who use a pole (see pages 24–25) do not need to cast. They push the end of the pole out to where they want to fish.

1 *Wind the line to one metre from the tip of the rod. Open the bale arm. Trap the line against the rod with your index finger so that no more line can come off the spool.*

An Overhead Cast with a Fixed Spool Reel

2 *Hold the end of the rod with your other hand. Take the rod back over your head.*

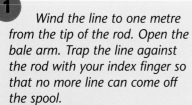

Things to Remember

The weight of the rig is what propels the line forward. A heavy rig will go further.

Before you cast, look around to make sure that there is no one behind you.

Try to avoid choosing an area where there are trees that might catch the line.

3 *Look directly at where you want the rig to land. Pull the bottom of the rod towards you and push the top towards the water – this will cast the rod forwards. Release the line trapped under your finger when the rod is at 45 degrees to the water.*

4 *When the bait hits the water, reel back until the line is tight.*

Carp

Appearance
There are three types of carp, the common (totally scaled), mirror (sparsely scaled) and leather (no scales) varieties. Carp can grow very large. Their colour can vary from dark brown to grey.

Where to find carp
The carp are found in rivers, canals, lakes reservoirs and even small ponds.

When to fish for carp
All year round but they are much more active in the summer months. The best time to fish for carp in the summer is at night.

How to fish for carp
Carp can be caught with most coarse fishing methods. Carp are mainly bottom feeders but in warmer weather they also feed on the surface.

Bait
Lobworms, redworms, maggots.

Hook
4–12

Line
6lb

Get Hooked!

Freelining is a natural method of fishing that uses the very minimum of equipment: a line, reel, hook and bait. To catch a fish as a freelining angler you need to understand and work with the flow of the river and the instincts of the fish.

Landing a Fish

Getting a fish to take the bait from your hook is only part of the skill of catching a fish. Until the fish has been carefully reeled in and landed on the bank there is still the possibility that it will escape.

Setting the Hook

When a fish has taken the bait, you need to set the hook in the fish's mouth to make sure of catching it. This is called the strike. You need to reel in any slack line and bring the tip of the rod up sharply. If you strike too quickly the hook may be jerked away from the fish. If you strike too slowly the fish may be gone.

This angler is about to bring his catch to the bank using a landing net.

▼

Playing the Fish

Once the strike has been made the fish is fighting for its life. It will put up all the resistance it can to being caught. Your next move is not as simple as just reeling in the line. If a powerful fish such as a pike or a large carp struggles on a taut line, the line will break and the fish will get way. To stop this happening you need to let out some line then reel it back in. Do this repeatedly until the fish has been gradually reeled in to the bank. This is called playing a fish.

Using the drag on your reel can help to increase the resistance and, as a result, tire out the fish.

Keep your rod low when you are playing a fish. Just before you land the fish, raise your rod and have your landing net ready.

Landing a Fish

A landing net is essential for bringing a fish to the bank. Remember to have the net close by so you can reach it. When you think the fish is exhausted, reel it in. Put the end of the landing net in the water and draw the fish towards it.

Taking out the Hook

If you can see the hook it may be possible to turn it and slide it out. If the hook is inside the mouth you will need to use a disgorger (see page 11) to get it out.

Catch and Release

Try to cause the fish as little stress as possible after it has been caught. Always handle a fish with wet hands or lay it on a damp fishing mat or wet grass. Fish have a slimy coating that protects their scales. This coating is damaged by contact with anything dry.

Return a fish to the water as quickly as you can once it has been measured, weighed and photographed. Hold it in the water for a few seconds until you feel it starting to swim before you let go.

Fishy Facts

A carp that lives in a gravelpit in Kent weighed 26.96kg when it was caught in 2001. The same fish, affectionately known as 'two-tone', weighed 27.10kg when it was caught in 2008. Who knows how big it will be next time!

This trout is being held in the water before being released. This is called nursing.

Pole Fishing

Pole fishing is becoming increasingly popular as an alternative to fishing with a rod and line. In pole fishing you use a long but very light carbon fibre or fibreglass pole instead of a rod. Pole fishing is suitable for all types of fishing environment from a fast-moving river to a still, small pond.

Fishing Pole Design

Fishing poles are between 6 and 18 metres long and are made up of sections that join together. The front sections have elastic running through them. The elastic comes in different strengths depending on the type of fish you are aiming to catch. The strength of elastic is matched to the weight of line you are using.

This angler is using a long fishing pole. It has a cup attachment at the end to sprinkle groundbait into the water before he starts to fish.

This angler is attaching a float and line to a fishing pole.

A pole is not cast, instead it is pushed out above the water until the rig at the end is in the right spot. Groundbait is placed in a cup that attaches to the end of the pole. The pole is pushed out into the position where the groundbait is needed. The groundbait is then tipped into the water. In this way you can deliver the bait precisely where you want it. Some poles are designed for catching big fish. Competition anglers say that using a pole can increase their catch considerably.

Holding a Pole

You use both hands to hold a pole when fishing. Hold the end of the pole out behind you with one hand, and with the other hand support the underside of the pole in front of you. Slide the pole forwards and backwards until you find the point where it is perfectly balanced. This will make it easier to hold for long periods of time.

Pole Floats

Pole floats are different from the floats used with a fishing rod. They are very light and have a slim streamlined design. They come in a range of sizes, colours and styles.

Catching a Fish

When a fish bites the float tip sinks down in the water. The hook is set (see page 22) by pushing down on the end of the pole which lifts the pole tip up in the air.

Tench

Appearance
The tench is a sturdily built fish with small scales. It has an olive green or bronze body and rounded fins. Its eyes are small and red and it has two fleshy whiskers called barbels, one either side of its mouth.

Where to find tench
At the bottom of still and slow-flowing waters, such as canals, lakes and slow-flowing rivers in most parts of Britain and across Europe and Asia.

When to fish for tench
Spring and summer at dawn and dusk

How to fish for tench
The most popular methods are float fishing with a waggler or a swimfeeder (see page 15).

Bait
Worms, maggots, sweetcorn, casters and bread.

Hook
Hook size 10 maximum. Always check fishery rules.

Line
6–8lb.

The Challenge of Fishing

Hooking and landing any fish can be a thrilling experience. You have read the water, found the fish, tempted it with the right bait, hooked it and played it successfully to the bank. Some people like to move on to greater challenges. This might mean trying to catch bigger fish or specialising in catching one particular species.

Match Fishing

Many anglers like to take part in fishing competitions. Clubs and societies organise match fishing to allow people to test their fishing skills against each other, in teams or in timed events.

At the beginning of the match, competitors are given their position or 'peg' and must fish from that spot for the duration of the match. As each person catches fish, they place them in a keep net in the water until the end of the day when the weight of all the fish is added together. The person with the highest total weight wins. Once the fish have been weighed they are returned to the water.

Competitions are held in teams as well as individually. Competing as part of a team can be a great help, as you can benefit from the experience of the other members. Many countries have national teams that compete against each other in international competitions. Some competitions are specific to a type of fish, such as carp, pike or to predatory fish in general.

▼ In a fishing match, competitors fish from the same place for the whole match.

 This pike has been caught using a lure. Lures are a shiny, brightly coloured, artificial bait. They are designed to look and act like injured fish to tempt predator fish to attack.

Pike

Appearance
A streamlined fish with a marbled grey, green and yellow pattern. A pike has vicious teeth on its upper and lower jaws as well as on the roof of its mouth and tongue.

Where to find pike
All sorts of places, such as canals, lakes, rivers and ponds in all parts of Britain and Europe. Pike hide amongst roots and in weeds waiting for their prey.

When to fish for pike
Spring and summer at dawn and dusk.

How to fish for pike
With a purpose built pike rod and a fixed-spool reel. You will need a large reel that can hold lots of heavy duty line. Floats used for pike fishing are large and heavy weights are needed to balance them in the water.

Hooks
Extra-strong hooks of size 4 to 8 are recommended.

Bait
Smaller pike and other small fish.

Fishing for Predators

Pike, zander and Wells catfish are predators that eat other smaller fish. They catch live fish or eat dead fish that have sunk onto the river bottom. They are big fish with sharp teeth. Catching and landing them can be a difficult and exhausting but very exciting experience. When predator fish have taken a hook they fight very hard to get away. Their sharp teeth can cut through ordinary line, so anglers use a fine wire called trace instead.

This marlin has finally been reeled in after an exhausting battle. It will be photographed before being returned to the sea.

Big Game Fishing

Fishing for monster salt water fish, such as the giant blue marlin, with a rod and line is called big game fishing. It is popular in oceans all over the world. Shark, marlin, and tuna are caught using specially adapted boats with experienced crews. These big fish are fearless and put up a real fight. Landing a blue marlin can be an hour of exhausting but exciting action.

Statistics and Records

Species	Kilos	Year	Location
Bream	8.90	2005	Cambridge Water
Carp	29.88	2005	Conningbrook Lake, Ashford
Catfish	28.123	1997	Withy Pool, Henlow, Bedfordshire
Chub	4.224	2007	Southern Stillwater
Dace	0.595	2002	River Weir
Eel	5.046	1978	Kingfisher Lake, Nr Ringwood, Hampshire
Perch	2.69	2006	Stillwater at Crowborough, Sussex
Pike	21.234	1992	Llandegfedd, Wales
Roach	1.93	2006	Northern Ireland Stillwater
Rudd	2.100	2001	Clay Lake, Co Armagh, NI
Zander	9.667	2007	River Severn at Upper Load Lock

World Records

Species	Kilos	Location	Country	Year
Common Carp	40.37	Les Graviers Lake	France	2007
Golden Perch	9.53	Lake Hume	Australia	1995
Roach	3.13	Rhine River	Germany	1981
Rudd	3.01	Danube River	Austria	1989
Tench	7.34	Lake in Herefordshire	England	1992

Glossary

Ancient Egyptians People who lived in Egypt between 3000 BCE and 400CE.

Bait Types of food used to catch fish.

Bite In fishing, this is the moment when a fish takes the bait on the hook.

Casting Throwing a fishing line out over the water to the correct spot using a rod and reel.

Freshwater Water in rivers and lakes that does not contain salt.

Groundbait A breadcrumb-like mixture which you scatter over the water to tempt fish into the area you are fishing.

Logging Writing down information to keep as a record.

Medicated wipe A cloth that has had a substance added to it that kills germs.

Prey An animal hunted for food.

Rig The combination of float, hook and line that you use when you fish.

Saltwater Water that contains salt. The water in the sea is saltwater.

Species A group of creatures with common features.

Strike The movement of the rod that makes sure the hook is secure in the fish's mouth.

Swim The area where you are fishing.

Swimfeeder A plastic tube with holes in it. In the water, bait is released through the holes to attract fish to the baited hook.

Tackle The equipment you need for fishing.

Trace Fine wire used instead of fishing line to catch predator fish, such as pike.

Vikings A group of Scandinavian people who lived between the eighth and tenth centuries.

Websites

http://www.discoverfishing. co.uk
As well as lots of useful information about fishing tackle, this site also has a directory of fishing clubs in the UK.

www.fishingexpert.co.uk
Information about coarse, game and sea fishing, as well as fishing for relaxation and for competition.

www.fishing.co.uk
This site has a lot of detailed information about all the species of fish you are ever likely to encounter.

www.environment-agency.gov.uk/homeandleisure/ recreation/default.aspx
Information about buying a rod licence, where to fish and how to get started.

www.netknots.com/html/fishing_ knots.html
Clear instructions and animated sequences help you to learn how to tie and use several different fishing knots.

Index